THE FORESTS

A Celebration of Nature, in Word and Image
Conceived and compiled by Michelle Lovric

COURAGE BOOKS

AN IMPRINT OF RUNNING PRESS
PHILADELPHIA · LONDON

9 8 7 6 5 4 3 2 1
Digit on the right indicates the number of this printing.

Library of Congress Cataloging-in-Publication Number 95–70140

ISBN 1–56138–507–7

Cover and interior design by Frances J. Soo Ping Chow.
Edited by Brian Perrin.

This book may be ordered by mail from the publisher.
But try your bookstore first!

Published by Courage Books,
an imprint of Running Press Book Publishers
125 South Twenty-second Street
Philadelphia, Pennsylvania 19103–4399

The compiler gratefully acknowledges the permission of the
following to reproduce copyrighted material in this book:

"The Fircone" and excerpt from "Beech Tree at Batsford
Arboretum" by Stephanie June Sorréll. Reproduced by permission
of the author. Copyright © 1995 Stephanie June Sorréll.

Excerpt from *The Book of a Naturalist* by William Henry Hudson,
published by Thomas Nelson & Sons Ltd. Reproduced by
permission of The Society of Authors as the literary representative
of the Estate of W. H. Hudson.

Excerpt from "Drowned in a Dream" by Michael Bullock from
Poems on Green Paper, published by Third Eye. Reproduced by
permission of the author. Copyright © 1988 Michael Bullock.

Excerpt from "Zacchaeus in the Leaves" by Vernon Watkins
from *Unity of the Stream,* published by Yr Academi Gymreig.
Reproduced by permission of Mrs. Gwen Watkins. Copyright
© 1978 Gwen Watkins.

Excerpt from "Sleepwalking Ballad" by Federico García Lorca,
translated by Kristina Blagojevitch. Translation copyright © 1996
Kristina Blagojevitch.

Excerpt from "Love Song" from *William Carlos Williams:
Collected Poems: 1909–1939,* Volume I. Reproduced by permission
of New Directions Publishing Corp. and Carcanet Press. Copyright
© 1938 New Directions Publishing Corp.

Excerpt from *The Tree* by John Fowles, published by Aurum.
Reproduced by permission of Sheil Land Associates. Copyright
© 1979 John Fowles.

"What I Want" by Nancy Cherry first published in *Green Fuse.*
Reproduced by permission of the author. Copyright © 1993
Nancy Cherry.

Excerpt from "For Forest" from *Lazy Thoughts of a Lazy Woman*
by Grace Nichols, published by Virago Press Ltd. Copyright
© 1984 Grace Nichols.

Excerpts from "Trees" from *The Collected Poems of Harold
Monro,* first published 1933 by R. Cobden, reprinted 1970 by
Gerald Duckworth & Co. Ltd. Reproduced by permission of
Gerald Duckworth & Co. Ltd.

Excerpt from "Symmetries and Asymmetries" from *The Collected
Poems of W. H. Auden,* edited by Edward Mendelsohn. Reproduced
by permission of Random House, Inc., and Faber and Faber Ltd.
Copyright © 1976 Edward Mendelsohn, William Meredith, and
Monroe K. Spears, Executors of the Estate of W. H. Auden.

INTRODUCTION

A forest is a living temple, a place that brings us as close as we can come to the potent beauty and deep mysteries of nature. We walk there in delight, but also in trepidation, for the forest embodies the fearsomeness, intensity, and awe of a religious experience.

It is a place in which we can seek not only shade and peace but also illumination. Its muffled dimness, dappled with a tantalizing tracework of filtered light, reaches out and touches all our senses. Each tree nourishes our soul and spirit. It is perhaps these qualities that have inspired so many architects to create places of worship according to the forest's primal design, with tall naves and variegated windows refracting and coloring the external light.

The forest is ancient and full of wisdom, yet innocent and green with newness. In the human psyche, it is garlanded with myth, history, and poetry. It is home to creatures both real and unreal—gentle birds and fierce wolves, fairies, nymphs, and witches. The sylvan glade and babbling brook speak of the peaceful, meditative life of the ascetic; but the forest's dark depths and hidden dangers are also the archetypal testing ground of heroes and warriors. The forest can be a place of ambush or a hallowed sanctuary, a place in which to be lost or a place in which to find oneself.

This book is a celebration of the magic and wonder of the forest, a collection of words and images to satisfy our longing for a return to a primeval world where the feel of the earth is familiar and we are part of its fruitful rituals.

TO THE EDGE OF THE WOOD I AM DRAWN, I AM DRAWN.

SIDNEY LANIER (1842–1881) AMERICAN POET

At the gates of the forest,

the surprised man

of the world is forced

to leave his city estimates

of great and small, wise and foolish.

The knapsack of custom

falls off his back.

RALPH WALDO EMERSON (1803—1892)
AMERICAN WRITER

I AM ANCIENT. PRIMEVAL.

BORN FROM THE EARTH'S DARK WOMB,

I AM SPUN FROM THE DUST OF THE STARS.

I BREATHE THE SLOW TIDES THAT SHAPE THE UNIVERSE.

I AM ANCIENT, BEAUTIFUL.

I HAVE PUSHED UP FROM SEED,

TO SAPLING AND MIGHTY BRANCHES.

I HAVE KNOWN THE ROAR OF SAP

IN MY VEINS, THE CARESS OF

BROTHER WIND AND THE SUN'S

BURNING KISS. THE BENEDICTION

OF THE SACRED RAINS HAVE REFRESHED

MY THIRST.

I AM ANCIENT, AWESOME.

WITHIN THE TIGHT NUGGET OF ME

I HOLD THE EARTH'S FERTILE DREAM.

HOLD ME AND YOU WILL KNOW

THAT MY PULSE IS YOUR PULSE.

BREATHE ME AND YOU WILL FIND

THE FRAGRANCE OF HEAVEN. AND

KNOW IT IN YOUR OWN BODY.

I AM ANCIENT.

I AM YOU. . . .

STEPHANIE JUNE SORRÉLL (B. 1956)
ENGLISH POET

FOR THE FOREST TREE KEEPS IN HER HEART SECRETS OF DAYS LONG GONE. . . .

Mary Webb (1881–1927) English novelist

THE FOREST IS TO ME THE SWEETEST COLLEGE. . . . WISDOM DOTH HERE IN ALL ITS BRANCHES GROW. . . .

Edward, Second Baron Thurlow (1781–1829) English poet

When one turned from the

lawns and gardens into the

wood it was like passing from

the open sunlit air to the

twilight and still atmosphere of

a cathedral interior.

WILLIAM HENRY HUDSON (1841–1922)

ENGLISH NATURALIST AND WRITER

Like two cathedral towers these stately pines

   Uplift their fretted summits tipped with cones;

The arch beneath them is not built with stones,

   Not Art but Nature traced these lovely lines, . . .

Enter! the pavement, carpeted with leaves,

   Gives back a softened echo to thy tread!

Listen! the choir is singing; all the birds,

   In leafy galleries beneath the eaves,

Are singing! listen, ere the sound be fled,

And learn there may be worship without words.

Henry Wadsworth Longfellow (1807–1882) American poet

For him the woods were a home and gave him the key

Of knowledge, thirst for their treasures in herbs and flowers.

The secrets held by the creatures nearer than we

To earth he sought, and the link of their life with ours:

And where alike we are, unlike where, and the veined

Division, veined parallel, of a blood that flows

In them, in us, from the source by man unattained

Save marks he well what the mystical woods disclose.

George Meredith (1828–1909) English poet and novelist

Let me stand in the
with great boughs all
about me. And just
glimpse of primeval
forgotten within this

heart of a beech tree,

sinewed and whorled

for a moment catch a

time that breathes

busy hurrying world.

STEPHANIE JUNE SORRÉLL (B. 1956) ENGLISH POET

Leaving behind the hot sun

I swim

into the cool womb of the wood . . .

rolling in a shallow sea

seaweed ferns

move gently in the flow

fallen trees

are sunken galleons

replete with treasure

I drift among the shifting shadows

drowned in a dream . . . .

MICHAEL BULLOCK (B. 1918)
ENGLISH-BORN CANADIAN POET

In the Forest silences throng. . . .

JOHN DAVIDSON (1837–1909)
SCOTTISH POET AND PLAYWRIGHT

A tree

Predestined to beauty.

Blown leaves

It is no exaggerated praise to call a tree the GRANDEST, and most BEAUTIFUL of all the productions of the earth.

WILLIAM GILPIN (1762–1843)
ENGLISH WRITER AND PAINTER

Antiquity.

Light lost. Light found.

Vernon Watkins (1906–1967)
Welsh poet

"Under the trees!" Who but agrees

That there is magic in words such as these?

CHARLES STUART CLAVERLEY (1831–1884)
ENGLISH POET

. . . IT IS NOT SO MUCH

FOR ITS BEAUTY

THAT THE FOREST

MAKES A CLAIM

UPON MEN'S HEARTS,

AS FOR THAT

SUBTLE SOMETHING,

THAT QUALITY OF THE AIR,

THAT EMANATION

FROM THE OLD TREES,

THAT SO WONDERFULLY

CHANGES AND RENEWS

A WEARY SPIRIT.

Robert Louis Stevenson (1850–1894)
Scottish writer

GREEN, I LOVE YOU GREEN.
GREEN WIND. GREEN BRANCHES.

Federico García Lorca (1898–1936)
Spanish poet and dramatist

I THINK THAT I SHALL NEVER SEE

A POEM LOVELY AS A TREE.

A TREE WHOSE HUNGRY MOUTH IS PRESSED

AGAINST THE EARTH'S SWEET FLOWING BREAST . . .

POEMS ARE MADE BY FOOLS LIKE ME,

BUT ONLY GOD CAN MAKE A TREE.

JOYCE KILMER (1886–1918)
AMERICAN POET

WHAT RICH TREES ARE ABOUT US,—ELMS, OAKS, AND BEECHES; NOT RICH IN FRUIT, BUT RICH IN VERDURE AND LEAVES, AND FOOD FOR POETRY.

JAMES HENRY LEIGH HUNT (1784—1859) ENGLISH ESSAYIST AND POET

I robbed the Woods—

The trusting Woods.

the unsuspecting Trees

Brought out their Burs and mosses

My fantasy to please.

I scanned their trinkets curious—

I grasped—I bore away—

What will the solemn Hemlock—

What will the Oak tree say?

Emily Dickinson (1830–1886)
American poet

In some mysterious way
woods have never seemed to me
to be static things. In physical
terms, I move through them;
yet in metaphysical ones,
they seem to move through me.

John Fowles (b. 1926)
English writer

THE ELM IS SCATTERING
ITS LITTLE LOAVES
OF SWEET SMELLS
FROM A WHITE SKY!

William Carlos Williams (1883–1963)
American physician and writer

My soul has mingled with the Forest's soul;

Danced with its lights and shadows; laughed its laugh;

Caught every lightest whisper as it stole; . . .

Breathed breath of bracken; heard what each tree said

To sun and wind and dew, and what each root

Said to the Earth, the dark eternal Mother;

What squirrel, mouse and hedgehog told each other

Of never-ending Summer; what the mole

Whispered to tree-root gnomes, deep in his hole;

Yea, heard the tale the robin and the wren,

The thrush, the blackbird, told his tiny hen:

Oh! I have listened to the warning wail

Of groping winds, precursors of the gale,

Between the shuddering oak-trees that well know

The battle-song of Tempest, and the roll

Of forest thunder, distant still and low:

My soul has mingled with the Forest's soul.

EUGENE LEE-HAMILTON (1845–1907)
ENGLISH POET AND NOVELIST

IN THE COUNTRY IT IS AS IF EVERY TREE SAID TO ME "HOLY! HOLY!" WHO CAN EVER EXPRESS THE ECSTASY OF THE WOODS?

Ludwig van Beethoven (1770–1827)
German composer

Why

are

there

trees

I

never

walk

under

but

large

and

melodious

thoughts

descend

upon

me?

Walt Whitman (1819–1892)
American poet

I WANT TO HEAD INTO THE WOODS WITH MY HANDS OPEN.

I WANT TO LOOK DOWN INTO A CANYON DUSTED IN WHITE

WITH BIRCH TREES RISING AMONG THE PINE

LIKE PLUMED ARROWS SHOT FROM THE RIDGE.

I WANT TO LIVE ON THE RIVER AND HEAR ICE COMING.

I WANT TO SLOW INTO THE HOLLOWS OF LOGS, SMELL

THE COLD WOODS, BARK AND GLACIER. I WANT TO HEAR

STORMS SHAKE SOUND FROM THE SKY, LET IT BOOM AROUND ME!

I WANT TO HEAR THE TREES SPEAK OF SNOW

WHILE I STAND IN MY DOORWAY, LISTENING.

Nancy Cherry (b. 1955)
American poet

LONG ROWS OF TREES AND WOODS MY PEN INVITE. . . .

John Evelyn (1655–1699) English writer

FOREST COULD KEEP SECRETS

FOREST COULD KEEP SECRETS

FOREST TUNE IN EVERYDAY

TO WATERSOUND AND BIRDSOUND

FOREST LETTING HER HAIR DOWN

TO THE TEEMING CREEPING OF HER FOREST GROUND

BUT FOREST DON'T BROADCAST HER BUSINESS

NO FOREST COVER HER BUSINESS DOWN

FROM SKY AND FAST-EYE SUN

AND WHEN NIGHT COME

AND DARKNESS WRAP HER LIKE A GOWN

FOREST IS A BAD DREAM WOMAN

FOREST DREAMING ABOUT MOUNTAIN

AND WHEN EARTH WAS YOUNG

FOREST DREAMING OF THE CARESS OF GOLD

FOREST ROOTSING WITH MYSTERIOUS ELDORADO

AND WHEN HOWLER MONKEY

WAKE HER UP WITH HOWL

FOREST JUST STRETCH AND STIR

TO A NEW DAY OF SOUND

BUT COMING BACK TO SECRETS

FOREST COULD KEEP SECRETS

FOREST COULD KEEP SECRETS

AND WE MUST KEEP FOREST

Grace Nichols (b. 1950) Guyanese writer

ONE IMPULSE FROM A VERNAL WOOD

MAY TEACH YOU MORE OF MAN,

OF MORAL EVIL AND OF GOOD

THAN ALL THE SAGES CAN.

William Wordsworth (1770–1850)
English poet

WE HAVE NOTHING TO FEAR AND A GREAT DEAL TO LEARN

FROM TREES, THAT VIGOROUS AND PACIFIC TRIBE WHICH

WITHOUT STINT PRODUCES STRENGTHENING ESSENCES FOR

US, SOOTHING BALMS, AND IN WHOSE GRACIOUS COMPANY

WE SPEND SO MANY COOL, SILENT AND INTIMATE HOURS.

Marcel Proust (1871–1922)
French novelist

As the leaves of the trees are said to absorb all noxious qualities of

the air, and to breathe forth a purer atmosphere, so it seems to me

as if they drew from us all sordid and angry passions, and breathed

forth peace and philanthropy. There is a severe and settled majesty

in woodland scenery that enters into the soul, and dilates and

elevates it, and fills it with noble inclinations.

Washington Irving (1783–1859)
American writer

They refresh the commonplaces of life, shed a harmony through the busy discord, and appeal to those first sources of emotion, which are associated with the remembrance of all that is young and innocent. They seem also to present us with a portion of the tranquillity we think we are labouring for.

JAMES HENRY LEIGH HUNT (1784–1859) ENGLISH ESSAYIST AND POET

One summer afternoon, you find

Some lonely trees. Persuade your mind

To drowse. Then, as your eyelids close,

And you still hover into those

Three stages of a darkening doze,

This side the barrier of sleep,

Pause. In that last clear moment open quick

Your sight toward where the green is bright and thick.

Be sure that everything you keep

To dream with is made out of trees.

Harold Monro (1879–1932)
English writer

Is there a thing more sweet

Than thus to sit—my feet

Deep in this forest-pool

So clear, and ah! so cool,

Hid from the sun-sick noon?

John Todhunter (1839–1916)
Irish doctor and poet

AND SOFTLY THRO' THE ALTERED AIR
HURRIES A TIMID LEAF.

Emily Dickinson (1830–1886):
American poet

. . . branches float on the wind more than they yield to it; and

in their tossing do not so much bend under a force, as rise on a

wave, which penetrates in liquid threads through all their sprays.

JOHN RUSKIN (1819–1900) ENGLISH WRITER AND CRITIC

THE

WIND

WALKS

WILDLY

IN

THE

TREES

TO-NIGHT.

Joseph Trumbull Stickney (1874–1904)
American poet

Slow swung the odorous trees from side to side,
Like censers, twining twilight mist for fume.

WILFRED OWEN (1893–1918)
ENGLISH POET

How still it is here in the woods. The trees

Stand motionless, as if they do not dare

To stir, lest it should break the spell. The air

Hangs quiet as spaces in a marble frieze.

Even this little brook, that runs at ease,

Whispering and gurgling in its knotted bed,

Seems but to deepen with its curling thread

Of sound the shadowy sun-pierced silences.

ARCHIBALD LAMPMAN (1861–1899)
CANADIAN POET

I remember, I remember
The fir-trees dark and high.

Thomas Hood (1799–1845)
English poet

Those green-robed senators of mighty woods,
Tall oaks, branch-charmed by the earnest stars,
Dream, and so dream all night without a stir. . . .
John Keats (1795–1821)
English poet

THE TREES THROW UP THEIR SINGING LEAVES, AND CLIMB

SPRAY OVER SPRAY. THEY BREAK THROUGH TIME.

THEIR ROOTS LASH THROUGH THE CLAY. THEY LAVE

THE EARTH, AND WASH ALONG THE GROUND;

THEY BURST IN GREEN WAVE OVER WAVE,

FLY IN A BLOSSOM OF LIGHT FOAM;

RANK FOLLOWING WINDY RANK THEY COME:

THEY FLOOD THE PLAIN,

SWILL THROUGH THE VALLEY, TOP THE MOUND,

FLOW OVER THE LOW HILL,

CURL ROUND

THE BASES OF THE MOUNTAINS, FILL

THEIR CREVICES, AND STAIN

THEIR RIDGES GREEN. . . .

Harold Monro (1879–1932) English writer

Deep in earth's opaque mirror,

The old oak's roots

Reflected its branches,

Astrologers in reverse,

Keen-eyed miners

Conned their scintillant gems. . . .

WYSTAN HUGH AUDEN (1907–1973)
ENGLISH-BORN AMERICAN POET

I SIGHED MY HEART INTO THE BOUGHS. . . . *Jean Ingelow (1820–1897) English poet*

That delicate forest flower,

With scented breath and look so like a smile,

Seems, as it issues from the shapeless mould,

An emanation of the indwelling Life,

A visible token of the upholding Love,

That are the soul of this great universe.

William Cullen Bryant (1794–1878)
American poet

. . . THE FOREST SMILES:
AND EVERY SENSE AND EVERY HEART IS JOY.

James Thomson (1700–1748)
Scottish poet

What does he plant who plants a tree?

He plants the friend of sun and sky;

He plants the flag of breezes free;

The shaft of beauty, towering high;

He plants a home to heaven anigh

For song and mother-croon of bird

in hushed and happy twilight heard—

The treble of heaven's harmony—

These things he plants who plants a tree.

Henry Cuyler Bunner (1855–1896)
American writer

HE THAT PLANTS TREES LOVES OTHERS BESIDE HIMSELF.
ENGLISH PROVERB

HE WHO PLANTS A TREE
PLANTS A HOPE.
LUCY LARCOM (1826—1893) AMERICAN POET

In wildness is the preservation of the world.

Henry David Thoreau (1817–1862)
American philosopher, writer, and naturalist

ILLUSTRATION ACKNOWLEDGMENTS

Front Cover; pp. 2-3, 24: *A Forest Glade,* Springtime, Johannes Boesen (Fine Art Photographic Library Ltd., No. JH2438)

Back Cover: *Springtime,* Christian Zacho (Fine Art Photographic Library Ltd., No. JH2459)

pp. 6-7: *Avenue, Evelyn Wood,* George Edmund Warren (Fine Art Photographic Library Ltd., No. TW3749)

p. 11: *A Pine Wood,* Autumn, Alfred Augustus Glendenning (Fine Art Photographic Library Ltd., No. TW6464)

p. 12: *Figures by a Woodland Stream,* Gustave Dore (Fine Art Photographic Library Ltd., No. TW5410)

p. 15: *Winter Sunset* (Fine Art Photographic Library Ltd., No.JH0302)

p. 19: *A Highland River,* William Mellor (Fine Art Photographic Library Ltd., No. FP0207)

pp. 20-21: *The Bluebell Walk,* Daniel Sherrin (Fine Art Photographic Library Ltd., No. FP1995)

pp. 22-23: *Where Tranquillity Lies,* Alfred Oliver (Fine Art Photographic Library Ltd., No. FP2132)

p. 27: *Figures in a Wooded River Landscape,* 1851, Barend Cornelius Koekkoek (Fine Art Photographic Library Ltd., No. AA1001)

pp. 28-29: *Cutting Logs,* Windsor Park, Windsor Castle in the Distance, Ralph W. Lucas (Fine Art Photographic Library Ltd., No. FP1432)

p. 30: *Deer in the Shade,* Joseph Denovan Adam (Fine Art Photographic Library Ltd., No. MK0101)

p. 33: *Still Waters,* Arthur H. Davis (Fine Art Photographic Library Ltd., No. FP1685)

p. 35: *The Woods in Silver and Gold,* Anders Andersen Lundby (Fine Art Photographic Library Ltd., No. FP0879)

pp. 36-37: *Duck Rising,* Peder Mork Monsted (Fine Art Photographic Library Ltd., No. FP2052)

pp. 38-39: *A Clearing in the Woods,* Thomas Bolton Gilchrist Septimus Dalziel (Fine Art Photographic Library Ltd., No. TW2618)

pp. 40-41: *A Forest Glade,* Carl Frederic Aagaard Hermansen (Fine Art Photographic Library Ltd., No. FP2401, and Bourne Gallery)

p. 42: *A Shady Stream,* Peder Mork Monsted (Fine Art Photographic Library Ltd., No. FP1906)

p. 45: *A Woodland Pool,* Olaf August Hermansen (Fine Art Photographic Library Ltd., No. FP2395, and Bourne Gallery)

pp. 46-47: *The Lake in the Woods,* 1891, Peder Mork Monsted (Fine Art Photographic Library Ltd., No. FP1165)

pp. 48-49: *A Mountain Peak with Drifting Clouds,* c. 1835, Caspar David Friedrich (Fine Art Photographic Library Ltd., No. AA494)

p. 51: *Winter Sunshine* (Fine Art Photographic Library Ltd., No. JH1194)

p. 52: *An Idyllic Landscape,* Kaisermann (Fine Art Photographic Library Ltd., No. AA3405)

p. 54-55: *Autumn Tints,* George Vicat Cole (Fine Art Photographic Library Ltd., No. TW4003)

p. 57: *An Alpine Landscape,* Adam Topffer (Fine Art Photographic Library Ltd., No. FP0973)

p. 58: *A View in Savernake Forest,* Wiltshire, Charles Leaver (Fine Art Photographic Library Ltd., No. FP2102)

p. 60: *The Deer Park,* J. Lewis (Fine Art Photographic Library Ltd., No. FP0897)

pp. 62-63: *Mont Blanc,* Edward Lear (Fine Art Photographic Library Ltd., No. TW1390)